How can a Smile Hide so much Pain?

Smiling while Dying on the Inside

By

Tracy B. Coney

Table of Contents

Dedication

This book is dedicated to the teachers and mentors who believed in me long before I learned to believe in myself.

To Ms. Nadine Wright Cook, Coach Willie B. Jackson, and Ms. Anita Bell Washington, thank you for seeing my potential when I could not, and for nurturing it with patience, discipline, and faith.

And to my brother, Dexter Miller, whose unwavering belief in me never faltered, your encouragement carried me through moments when I needed it most.

My work exists because of you.

Acknowledgment

Writing a book is hard. It is hard because you have to relive moments from the past that can be hurtful, painful, and sometimes even exciting. Bringing these memories back to life was not always easy, but it was necessary for me to tell my story honestly and with love.

First, I thank God for giving me the strength to write this book. God never left my side through every disappointment and every accomplishment. He carried me when I was weak, encouraged me when I was tired, and reminded me that my story mattered.

I thank all of my teachers, starting with Barbara Lee Williams, who is featured in the photo in this book. She never treated any of us differently. She treated us all the same, and it was her love, patience, and kindness that helped shape me into who I am today.

I thank my brother, Dexter Miller, who has always encouraged me and reminded me how proud he is of me. He has always had my back throughout life, and I am truly grateful for his constant support.

I would also like to thank Ms. Rosie Brown, who was a teacher assistant. She made clothes for us, gave us reading lessons, and pushed us to keep going no matter what. She has always believed in me and wanted to see me succeed. She even plans to buy the first copy of this book. She turned eighty on January 29, 2026, and continues to be a blessing in my life.

To my Dearest Mom, Pauline Scott. Thank you for bringing me into this world. No matter what the odds were stacked against you. You Did It, Lady. You have always been my Shining Star, throughout my life. I will Forever Love You, Pauline Scott.

To my sisters, Donna Scott and Lisa Hall, who stayed up many nights listening to me break down and helped me gather my thoughts, thank you for always being there when I needed you most.

To my children, Whittney Kilgore, D'Army Williams, Brittany Stevenson, Pauleaner Anderson, and Mya Bank, thank you for always following in my footsteps and showing me how much you love me. You are my greatest blessings, and everything I do is for you.

To my classmates and teachers, Kimberly Frazier, Twilla Smith, Natalie Stribling, and Quinton Jackson, thank you all for being there for me through it all.

Your support and friendship meant more to me than you may ever know.

To my special friends, Vivian Bradford and Alice Jackson. Thank you for always cheering me on, and for always being there for me. I love you both.

Thank you to the editors, Fionn, Rachael, Jack, and everyone involved, for the magnificent work you have done. Your dedication and care helped bring this book to life, and I truly appreciate each of you.

To the Readers,

Thank you from the bottom of my heart for purchasing this book. Thank you for the love you have shown me over the years, for reading my posts on Facebook, and for supporting me from near and far. God has a blessing with your name on it. I pray this book motivates you to find the strength to keep going and to make your dreams happen, no matter what. I love you all.

Preface

How many times have you looked at someone and said to yourself, *wow, she's pretty, she has a good life*? How many times have you passed people in and out of stores, on the job, at church, at outings, or seen them on social media and thought, *I want to be like her*? In life, it often feels like somebody else is always doing better than you.

Somebody else is happier.

Somebody else is stronger.

Somebody else has it all together.

At least, that's how it looks.

But do you ever stop to think about how many people are out here just trying to survive the cards they've been dealt? How many are smiling on the outside while silently wondering every day if they have the strength to keep going?

I'll tell you, there are too many to count.

Everyone is different. Some people believe that being liked will finally make them feel worthy. Some think popularity will fill the empty spaces inside them.

Some convince themselves that being noticed means being loved, yet nothing ever truly changes. And still, we keep reaching for approval from people who don't care about us.

Why do we do that? Why do we measure ourselves against lives we don't even know? Why do we judge our worth based on people who may be struggling just as much as we are, or more?

It's called *"on the outside looking in."*

We see the smiles.

We see the filters.

We see the success.

We see the confidence.

What we don't see are the breakdowns. The rejection. The loneliness. The nights spent crying and praying for things to be different. Life shows us the polished version of people, but it skips everything it took for them to get there.

That is why the saying *"never judge a book by its cover"* is so true.

This book is about a young girl who went through ups and downs, disappointments, and belittling.

A girl who cried many tears. Who was made fun of and laughed at. Who was told she would never be nothing. Who was called bald-headed for years. Called ugly. Called **"crazy like your mama."** Called poor. And worse.

Words that cut deep.

Words that stay with you.

Words that can change how you see yourself.

This is her story, not just about pain, but about endurance. Not just about being broken, but about learning how to stand again. It is about what happens when the world tries to define you, and you have to decide whether to accept it… or fight back.

If you have ever felt invisible, overlooked, misunderstood, or unworthy, this book is for you.

You are not alone. Dedication

This book is dedicated to the teachers and mentors who believed in me long before I learned to believe in myself.

To Ms. Nadine Wright Cook, Coach Willie B. Jackson, and Ms. Anita Bell Washington, thank you for seeing my potential when I could not, and for nurturing it with patience, discipline, and faith.

And to my brother, Dexter Miller, whose unwavering belief in me never faltered, your encouragement carried me through moments when I needed it most.

My work exists because of you.

Chapter 1:

Behind the Smile

At a very young age, there were so many days when I would put on a smile to hide the pain I was going through. As a child, I learned how to smile even when I was hurting, how to pretend everything was okay, how to cover the scars that came from being talked about each day when I got on the school bus. I learned early that sometimes smiling was the only way to survive.

I was born in a small town called Elaine, Arkansas. I was delivered by a midwife, an older lady whom I would later grow up to sing in the choir with. Life has a funny way of bringing things full circle like that. I was the third out of four children, trying to find my place in a world that already felt confusing and uncertain.

At the age of two, my grandparents got custody of us because my mother became ill, something that would later be called a *"nervous breakdown."* As a child, that was the word people used around me, and it felt like everyone at school knew about it. It followed me. It became part of how others saw me before they ever really knew me.

For some unknown reason, my hair would not grow. It stayed very short. My grandmother tried everything to help it grow, hoping something would work, but nothing ever did.

So each day I went to school, I already knew what was waiting for me. The other kids were ready. Ready to laugh. Ready to point. Ready to call me *"bald-headed Tracy."*

Those words hurt more than people realize. They made me feel ashamed, angry, sad, and confused all at once. It became part of my everyday life.

When my grandmother took us in, she already had nine children, including my mom. I know now how hard that must have been for her. She carried so much responsibility on her shoulders.

We lived in a three-bedroom house with a back porch that had no windows. There were five square spaces cut out for windows, but they were never put in. Light tried to come in, but it never quite made it all the way.

At night, my bed was the floor.

A cold, hard floor, with only two blankets to cover up. And keep in mind, the house only had one bathroom. It would be years before I had a bed to call my own. When my uncles and aunts grew up and moved out, it finally became my turn. Even though I had to share it with my two sisters, we were just happy to be off the floor.

Every day at school, the teasing continued. Because of my short hair, I was often mistaken for a boy. Oh, how it hurt deep down inside. It crushed parts of me that I didn't even know how to name yet. Still, I smiled and went on.

I had all the qualities of a girl, the hips, the legs, the waistline, yet no hair. That one thing made life so much harder than it needed to be.

One of my greatest challenges came when I wanted to be on the Royalettes Drill Team. I could twirl the baton better than anyone. I had the shape to fit the uniform. I had the ability. I had the heart.

But I didn't have hair.

One day, my teacher pulled me aside. She told me she really wanted me to be part of the team. She believed in me. But she also knew that when we traveled to games, cruel children might embarrass me by making fun of me in a skirt or dress.

She was trying to protect me.

Still, it hurt.

Moments like that taught me how to smile even harder. How to hide deeper pain. The pain of feeling rejected. Shut out. Not good enough. Unwanted.

So at school, I kept my head up. I acted strong. I pretended I was okay.

But when it was time to get on the bus, I would look out of the window and cry.

Quiet tears. Lonely tears.

Even now, thinking about it, tears still run down my face like rain. Some memories never fade. I was too ashamed to tell my siblings. I didn't want them to worry. I didn't want to seem weak.

So I carried it alone.

And I kept smiling.

Chapter 2:

For One Day, I was Brave

As the months passed, another teacher asked me if I could participate in the assembly program. When she asked me, my heart felt full, but I also felt scared. I had to go home and ask my grandmother if I could sing with my class at the program. When I asked her, she said no. She told me to just stay at home the day of the program.

I was disappointed, but I didn't say much.

I still went to practice at school, and my teacher told me she would bring me a dress, shoes, and a hair bow. The next morning, my grandmother was sick and had forgotten that I had asked her about the program. My heart was beating fast, but I made a decision. I sneaked out of the house and went on to school.

That day, I put the dress on. I fixed myself the best I could. I stood with my class, recited my scripture, and sang. Nobody said anything bad to me. At least, not to my face.

Boy!! Boy!! Boy!!

When I got home, all the children told my grandmother, *"Tracy was on the assembly program at school today, and she had a dress on and new shoes and a bow in her head."* My heart dropped. I knew I was in trouble.

My grandmother said, "I told you not to go, and you went anyway." Then she asked, "What did you do?"

I told her, *"I had a scripture to read from Ecclesiastes, the 3rd chapter."*

"To everything there is a season, and a time to every purpose under heaven..."

A time to be born, and a time to die.

A time to plant, and a time to pluck up.

A time to heal.

A time to build up.

A time to weep.

A time to laugh.

A time to mourn.

A time to dance.

A time to lose.

A time to keep.

A time to cast away.

After I finished, my grandmother looked at me and said, "You learned all of that?"

I bowed and replied, "Yes ma'am."

She didn't say anything else.

At the program, I got a standing ovation. My grandmother missed out seeing me perform. She could've been there to clap or root for me, but she wasn't. She never came to anything for me. I was always alone on every stage in my life. Nobody showed up for me. Nobody from my family clapped for me. Even then, she did not clap or speak. She just nodded her head.

But somehow, that meant everything.

On the inside, I was so happy I didn't know what to do. For once, I had done something that showed another side of me. A side that had been trying to break through all the pain. I never knew how my teacher got that bow to stay in my head until the program was over, but that day, I felt loved in my own way.

For the first time in a long time, nobody teased me. Nobody made me feel ashamed. Nobody laughed at my hair. I realized that the scripture I had recited was more than just words. It felt like God was speaking to me. It felt like I was coming alive, even if only for one day.

My tears were tears of joy, not sadness.

It was a time for me to be brave.

In some strange and beautiful way, God used my teachers to guide me in a direction I never thought existed. That one program was only the beginning. After that, my grandmother never said another word about me being in assemblies.

But life didn't suddenly become easy.

As the months passed, I went into the cafeteria with my class for lunch one day. The high school students would always come in before we finished eating. They stood around the walls, loud and laughing, teasing everybody, especially me.

That day, my uncle was in line. One of his friends said, *"Scott Mane, ain't that your niece?"*

My uncle said, *"Hell no, that's not my niece."*

I was sitting right there.

I heard him.

The pain went through me like a bullet. Right in front of my face, he denied me. I tried to smile. I tried to hold it together. But my face watered, and I hurried out of the cafeteria.

From that day on, I stopped eating there. I felt like he was ashamed of me, when he had a bed and I had slept on the floor.

Once again, I fell back into depression. I felt unwanted. Unloved. Betrayed. Ugly. Bald-headed. All the names came back. Some days, I tried to smile, but my smile wouldn't come alive. If my own family felt that way, what did others think?

I stopped eating at school. I stayed hungry until it was time to go home.

One day in class, I couldn't hold my pee any longer and had an accident in my school clothes. The teacher sent me to the office, and they gave me new clothes. I asked the lady if I had to bring them back. She said, *"No, they're yours."*

In my child's mind, I thought, *if this happens again, maybe I'll have better clothes. Maybe they'll stop picking on me.*

It happened again. And again.

I built a small wardrobe. The teasing slowed down. I cherished those clothes. I ironed them. I got up early. I prepared myself.

Because for the first time, I felt like I had something to be proud of.

Chapter 3:
One Step at a Time

By the end of fourth grade, my hair had finally started to grow. By seventh grade, it was about two to three inches long. To some people, that might not seem like much, but to me, it meant everything. It meant hope. It meant change. It meant that maybe, just maybe, I wouldn't be laughed at so much anymore.

My grandmother let the lady next door put a Jeri curl in my hair. It was not too short to roll, and for the first time in a long time, I felt like I was starting to look like the girl I always knew I was inside. When I got on the bus that day, I held my head up a little higher. I felt different. I felt seen.

The next year, my hair was different, and I didn't look so much like a boy anymore. The teasing eased up a little. Here and there, some still made fun of me, but it wasn't as cruel as before. It didn't cut as deep. Slowly, I started to feel better about myself. I started to believe that I wasn't as ugly as they said. I started to believe that I mattered.

One day, I saw a sign that said Basketball Tryouts. Something inside me stirred. I felt excited and scared at the same time. I went home and told my grandmother, and she quickly said, *"You don't have money for none of that."* She didn't even know what I was good at from playing in P.E. She didn't know how fast I could run, how hard I tried, or how badly I wanted it.

When the coach asked me if I was going to try out, I told him my grandma already said she didn't have money for shoes and that she wasn't going to pick me up from practice. Saying it out loud hurt. It made my dream feel small and impossible.

To make a long story short, the coach knew my grandmother because his brother lived two houses down the street, and he had gone to school with my uncles. God was already working behind the scenes, even when I couldn't see it.

One day, the coach showed up at our door and asked her if he bought the shoes and brought me home from practice, could I play. Lord have mercy, my grandma said, *"Yes, she can play."* I was so happy, I almost cried right there.

But after he left, she called me in and said she knew I had asked him to come over and talk to her.

I told her, *"No ma'am, I never asked him. He asked me, and I told him you said you didn't have any money."*

That was the truth. I didn't know how to beg for blessings. I just told my story.

After many evenings of practice, we were ready for our first game. I worked hard. I pushed myself. I showed up even when I was tired, even when I felt like quitting.

When I made it to the game, Coach gave me my bag with my shoes in it. I went to the dressing room, and everyone was getting dressed. My heart was beating fast. When I opened the box, I started crying. Coach had bought me low-top Nikes, and everyone else had high-top shoes on.

I felt different again. I felt out of place.

I cried so much until one of the senior girls came into the dressing room and asked what size I wore. Her name was Vickie Montague. Without hesitation, she let me wear her brand-new shoes for my first game. She didn't judge me. She didn't laugh. She just helped me.

It was unbelievable. This was very new for someone like me who had faced nothing but cruelty all my childhood.

Look at God, how He worked it out in my favor! I exclaimed in my mind.

The next game, Coach had gotten me the right shoes to wear. When I put them on, I felt proud. I felt stronger. I felt like I belonged.

Still, I smiled to hide my pain of not having the money to buy my own shoes. Behind that smile was a little girl who knew what it felt like to go without. A little girl who learned early how to be grateful and hurt at the same time.

But that season taught me something powerful.

It taught me that even when I had nothing, God would always make a way.

And little by little, I was learning to walk in confidence. One step at a time.

Chapter 4:

When I Really Saw Myself

After a few years passed, I made it to 9th grade. By then, I had already been through so much, but I was still standing. My history teacher was so nice. She truly had the best class. Her name was Miss Nadine Wright. This teacher dressed so nice, everything was always matching, and she wore some nice perfume that filled the room when she walked in.

All of us wanted to be like her. She carried herself with confidence, kindness, and grace, and without even realizing it, she was becoming someone I looked up to.

One day, she sent for me to come to her class. I was in another class, and she sent a note asking me to come see her during my lunch break. When I walked in, I was nervous. I didn't know what I had done wrong. But instead of correcting me, she smiled and asked me if I could tutor her daughter in math.

She told me she had been watching me. She said I was making good grades. She knew I had been raised by my grandparents, and she shared that she was a single parent. She believed that maybe I could help her daughter. What that moment did for me and my life, I could never fully explain.

My heart hurried, and I quickly said, *"Yes ma'am. I would love to help your daughter."*

What my teacher didn't know was that she was building me up. She was opening my eyes to something I never knew was possible. For the first time, I was starting to see my worth. Someone saw something in me before I fully saw it in myself. It took God placing these teachers in my path, one after another, so that I wouldn't give up on myself.

All my life, I have seen and felt God's hand on me, even when I wasn't doing right, even when I felt forgotten. I can still feel His presence watching over me, guiding me, protecting me, and reminding me that my story was not over.

My teacher's daughter ended up getting a B in her math class. It has been years since then. Today, she has two children and is grown, living an amazing life with her husband and her two sons. And every time I think about that, I smile, knowing I was a small part of her journey too.

That same year, another teacher asked me to be the homecoming queen for our class. I told her, *"I know my grandmother is not going to say yes."* She had too many children to take care of, and I knew she wasn't going to buy me a dress and all the things I would need. In my mind, it already felt impossible.

But God had another plan.

One day, somebody knocked on our door. It was my teacher, Ms. Donna Ross. She came to our house to ask my grandmother if I could run for homecoming queen. Before my grandmother could even say no, Ms. Donna Ross spoke up and said, *"I am going to buy everything she needs if she wins."*

My grandmother couldn't say no after that.

Y'all… we won.

We raised the most money, and I became the homecoming queen.

It was one of the happiest days of my childhood.

Ms. Donna Ross bought me the prettiest dress I had ever seen in my life. She bought my shoes, earrings, and jewelry. She even let me borrow her mink stole fur. Oh my God, it was beautiful. I had never owned anything so nice before. I felt like a princess.

That night, I wore a long train that was green and white, our school colors, and it flowed behind me everywhere I walked. The captain of the senior boys' basketball team crowned me and kissed me on the jaw. Lord, I almost fainted.

Calvin Thomas, who lived up the street from me, crowned me and asked if my crown was on right. I said yes. I smiled so hard and so nervously until the night was over.

For the first time in my life, I really looked at myself in a picture and saw something different. I saw confidence. I saw strength. I saw beauty. I noticed my smile in a way I never had before. Maybe it was because it had never been lit up like that before.

That night, my tears were not from pain.

They were tears of joy.

They came from feeling loved, confident, proud, and accomplished. From knowing that I mattered. From knowing that I belonged.

That night, I represented Miss C. V. White High with class and grace.

And for once in my life, I truly believed I deserved to be there. It was God's grace for letting me see a day like that in my life.

As I look back on all these moments, I realize that it was my teachers who kept standing in the gap for me when life felt heavy and unfair. When I didn't see my own worth, they saw it for me.

When I felt small, invisible, or unsure, they spoke life into me and reminded me that I mattered. They didn't just teach me lessons from books, they taught me how to believe in myself, how to walk with confidence, and how to hold my head up even when my heart was hurting.

Through their kindness, their patience, and their faith in me, they helped shape the woman I was becoming. I carry their love, encouragement, and sacrifices with me to this day.

I will forever be grateful for every teacher who chose to see something special in a little girl who was still learning how to see it in herself.

Chapter 5:

Smiling Through It All

Many times throughout my young life, it was very hard. So hard that there were days I wanted to crawl under a rock and disappear. Days when I felt like everyone was laughing at me. Days when I felt like I didn't belong anywhere.

Many days I thought I wouldn't be nothing. So many days I almost believed what the naysayers had to say about me, that I was crazy like my mama, ugly, poor, bald-headed, and that I wasn't going to amount to much in life.

Those words hurt. They stayed in my heart. Sometimes they followed me to bed at night. Sometimes they were the first thing I thought about when I woke up in the morning. There were moments when I really started to see myself the way they saw me. Small. Broken. Not enough.

But even in my weakest moments, when I was tired of being strong, when my smile felt heavy on my face, God never left me alone.

Every time I would get down on myself, God always put somebody in my path to brighten my day. Someone would show up at just the right time; a teacher, a coach, a kind voice, a helping hand, to remind me that I mattered. Someone always showed up to cheer me on, to tell me to keep pushing, even when I didn't believe in myself anymore.

Looking back now, I see that God was speaking to me through people long before I ever understood it.

All of us have something that is amazing about us. Every single one of us. Sometimes it's buried under hurt. Sometimes it's hidden under shame. Sometimes it's covered by fear. And not all the time will people see it in you. Some people will only see your struggle and never your strength.

But God has His own way of leading and guiding you into your destiny.

Even when you feel lost.

Even when you feel forgotten.

Even when you feel like giving up.

You have the last say over who you become in life. God first, and then it's up to you to decide who you will be.

Never let anyone label you. Never let anyone define your future by your past. Never let anyone convince you that you are less than what God created you to be.

Only you can decide who you will become.

Today, I thank God for every hard time.

Every disappointment.

Every bad day.

Every crying day.

Every uphill and downhill day.

Because it was all of those trials and tears that He used to shape me. It was all of those lonely nights and broken moments that built the woman I am today. Nothing was wasted. Nothing was for nothing.

God was working even when I couldn't see it.

Today, after all those years of pain and praying, I stand proud of how far I've come. From a cosmetologist of 33 years, to earning my Master's in Public Administration, to owning a restaurant, a beauty shop, an event hall, and a community playground, God has exceeded every dream I was too afraid to speak out loud.

And at the age of 55, I am still growing. Still learning. Still reaching. Still believing. I am working toward my second Master's in Social Work, to be completed in 2027 or earlier, because my story is not finished yet.

I am living proof that your beginning does not decide your ending.

Always remember, everyone has a story. And someone out there needs to hear yours. Someone is waiting for your testimony. Someone is praying for the strength that you already carry inside of you.

My prayer is that as you read this book, you felt my pain.

My prayer is that you feel my tears.

My prayer is that you walked with me through my storms.

And most of all, my prayer is that in the end, you too gained confidence to pursue whatever your dreams are.

Behind many smiles is so much pain. Behind many *"I'm okay"* moments are silent battles nobody sees. But sometimes it's that very pain that keeps you pushing. Sometimes it's your struggle that prepares you for your purpose.

To all those out there, heartbroken, bullied, hurting, your tears were not wasted. Your prayers were heard. Your strength was noticed.

This is your time. Your time to heal. Your time to grow. Your time to rise. Your time to receive what God has for you.

Keep smiling.

Keep believing.

Keep going.

Author's Note

As I come to the end of this book, my heart is full in ways that are hard to put into words. Writing my childhood journey has taken me back to places I hadn't visited in years, moments of pain, shame, confusion, and moments

When I questioned my worth and my purpose. There were times while writing this that I had to pause, wipe my tears, and pray, because reliving some of these memories was not easy. But I knew in my spirit that this story needed to be told.

This book is not about perfection. It is about survival. It is about faith. It is about learning how to smile when your heart is breaking, how to stand when you feel like falling, and how to keep going when everything in you wants to quit. For many years, I hid my pain behind a smile.

I learned how to look strong even when I was weak. I learned how to say *"I'm okay"* when I was hurting inside. But God saw every tear, every silent prayer, and every lonely night. And He never left me.

I share my story not for sympathy, but for strength. I want you to know that no matter where you come from, no matter what you have been through, no matter what people have said about you, your life still has meaning.

Your dreams are still valid. Your future is still bright. Your mistakes do not cancel your purpose. Your struggles do not disqualify you from greatness. If God brought me through, He can bring you through too.

Throughout my life, God used people, teachers, mentors, family members, and even strangers to remind me that I was worth more than I believed. He placed helpers in my path when I was tired. He sent encouragers when I was discouraged.

He opened doors when I thought all hope was gone. Looking back now, I can see His hand on me even in moments when I didn't understand what He was doing. Every delay, every closed door, every heartbreak had a purpose.

If you are reading this and you are hurting, I want you to know that you are not alone. If you are struggling to believe in yourself, I want you to know that God still believes in you.

If you feel forgotten, overlooked, or unworthy, please remember that God specializes in using the broken, the rejected, and the overlooked to do great things.

Your story is not over.

Your best days are still ahead.

Thank you for trusting me with your time, your heart, and your emotions as you read my story. Thank you for walking with me through my journey. Thank you for allowing my testimony to touch your life.

My prayer is that this book gave you hope, courage, and the strength to keep going, no matter what you are facing.

Always remember: *behind every smile is a story. Behind every strong person is a journey. And behind every victory is a God who never gave up on you.*

With love and gratitude,

Tracy B. Coney

About the Author

Tracy writes from a life shaped by storms, faith, disappointment, and resilience, all woven together into a powerful testimony of strength and perseverance. Drawing from real-life experiences, she writes with honesty and heart, inviting readers into a journey that shows how hope can rise even in the darkest seasons of life.

Her work brings spiritual truth, encouragement, and inspiration to those seeking strength, healing, and motivation. Through her words, she reminds readers that they are never alone and that their struggles do not define their future.

Guided by a deep belief in the power of faith, Tracy shares her story to encourage others to keep going, trust God's plan for their lives, and embrace the possibility of transformation. Her voice is authentic, uplifting, and rooted in the belief that every challenge can be overcome with faith, courage, and perseverance.

When she is not writing, Tracy continues to inspire others through social media, within her community, and through everyday conversations. She is deeply committed to encouraging people to keep moving forward, becoming the best version of themselves, and remembering that they are worthy, valued, and loved.